Siwon's Story of
American Presidents II

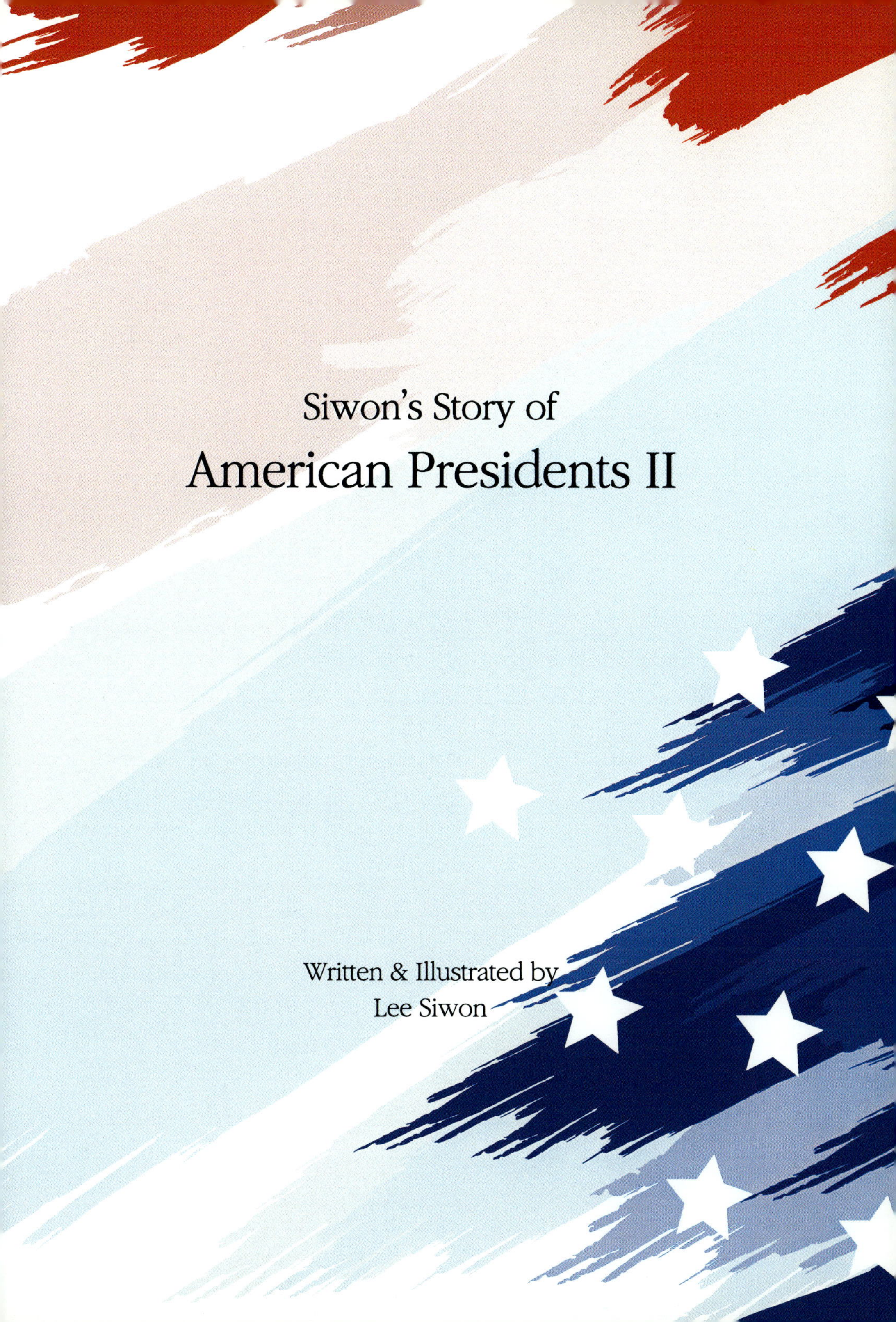

Siwon's Story of

American Presidents II

Written & Illustrated by
Lee Siwon

Prologue

Hello, my name is Siwon and I am 11years old. I like to research and learn about politics and economics. I wrote this book which is a sequel to my first book: Siwon's Story of American Presidents. Many of my friends and family enjoyed the story so it gave me courage and inspiration to write another one.

This story focuses on different presidents and new topic: presidents who lead the cold war, who served in the military, and those who were assassinated. While I was researching, I realized that being a president is not an easy job. I hope that readers of this book also realize the importance of their existence, and the hard work they did to make America proud.

May 26th, 2021

Written & Illustrated by Lee Siwon.

Contents

Part I.

Seven American Presidents

Who Led the Cold War

There were seven American presidents who led the Cold War. They are Harry S. Truman, Dwight David Ike Eisenhower, John Fitzgerald Jack Kennedy, Lyndon Baines Johnson, Richard Milhous Nixon, Gerald Rudolph Ford Jr. and Ronald Wilson Reagan.

Illustrated by Lee Siwon

Harry S. Truman
(1884. 5. 8 ~ 1972. 12. 26)

First, Harry S. Truman was the 33rd president of the U.S. He was born on May 8th, 1884. He ended World War II by launching two atomic bombs to Japan. He was the first president who led the Cold War. Then, he supported the Korean War. He was the 11th president that was a former vice president. Also, he was the 7th president to succeed his presidency.

Before he became a president, he was the vice president of the U.S. for three months. Then, he was the president from 1945 to 1953.

Illustrated by Lee Siwon

Dwight David Ike Eisenhower
(1890. 10. 14 ~ 1969. 3. 28)

Second, Dwight David Ike Eisenhower was the 34th president of the U.S. He was born on October 14th, 1890. He was a hero of World War II. Also, he ended the Korean War with the UN.

He was 6th president who was a former soldier. Then, he was the second president who led the Cold War. Before he became a president, He was the Captain General of the European Union for one year. Then, he was the president of the U.S. from 1953 to 1961.

Illustrated by Lee Siwon

John Fitzgerald Jack Kennedy
(1917. 5. 29 ~ 1963. 11. 22)

Third, John Fitzgerald Jack Kennedy was the 35th president of the U.S. He was born on May 29th, 1917. He ended the nuclear war against the Soviet Union.

He was the 4th president to be assassinated. The assassinator was Lee Harvery Oswald. Also, he was the 3rd president who led the Cold War. Before he became a president, He was the senator of the U.S. from 1953 to 1960. Then, he was the president of the U.S. for 2 years and 10 months.

Illustrated by Lee Siwon

Lyndon Baines Johnson
(1908. 8. 27 ~ 1973. 1. 22)

Fourth, Lyndon Baines Johnson was the 36th president of the U.S. He was born on August 27th, 1908. He fought with north Vietnam during the Vietnam War. He was the 12th president that was a former vice president. Also, he was the 8th president to succeed his presidency. He was the 4th president who led the Cold War. Before he became a president he was the vice president of the U.S. for two years. Then, he was the president of American from 1963 to 1969.

Illustrated by Lee Siwon

Richard Milhous Nixon
(1913. 1. 9 ~ 1994. 4. 22)

Fifth, Richard Milhous Nixon was the 37th president of the U.S. He was born on January 9th, 1913. He ended the Vietnam War. Also, he became the first president to resign during his presidency.

That was all because of Watergate Scandal. He was the 5th president who led the Cold War. Before he became a president, he was a vice president of the United States from 1953 to 1961. Then, he was the president of America from 1969 to 1974.

Illustrated by Lee Siwon

Gerald Rudolph Ford Jr.
(1913. 7. 14 ~ 2006. 12. 26)

Sixth, Gerald Rudolph Ford Jr. was the 38th president of the U.S. He was born on July 14th, 1913. He was the 9th president to succeed his presidency. Also, he was the 13th president that was a former vice president.

He was the 15th president who lost his re-election. Before, he became a president, he was a vice president of the U.S. for one year. And he was the 6th president who led the Cold War. Then, he was the president of America from 1974 to 1977.

Illustrated by Lee Siwon

Ronald Wilson Reagon
(1911. 2. 6 ~ 2004. 6. 5)

Last, Ronald Wilson Reagon was the 40th president of the United States. He was born on February 6th, 1911. He was the last president who led the Cold War. He was the first president who was an actor. Also, he was the 8th president who was a governor. He ended the cold war and brought down the Soviet Union. Before he became a president, he was the governor of California state from 1967 to 1975. Then, he was the president of America from 1981 to 1989.

In conclusion, these are the seven American presidents who led the Cold War. Among these leaders, I like Ronald Wilson Reagon the most. The reason is because he ended the Cold War and pulled down the Soviet Union.
All of these presidents have left a positive impact on the development of America as a country.

Part II.

Six American Presidents

Who were Soldiers

There are six American presidents that were soldiers : George Washington, Andrew Jackson, William Henry Harrison, Zachary Taylor, Ulysses Simpson Grant, and Dwight David Ike Eisenhower.

Illustrated by Lee Siwon

George Washington
(1732. 2. 22 ~ 1799. 12. 14)

George Washington was the first president of the U.S.
He was born on Feburary 22nd, 1732. When he died, many American called him the "Father Of Our Country." He was the first president elected by the electroral college.

Also, he was the first American president who was a soldier. He was a hero of the American Independence War. Before he became a president, he was the first speaker of National Assembly from 1783 to 1789. Then, he was the president of the U.S. from 1789 to 1797.

Illustrated by Lee Siw

Andrew Jackson
(1767.3.15 ~ 1845.6.8)

Andrew Jackson was the 7th president of the U.S. He was born on March 15th, 1767. He was the hero of the second war with the U.K.

Many Americans called him "Old Hickory." Also, he was the second president that was a soldier. Before he became a president, he was the senator of the U.S for 2 years. Then, he was the president of America from 1829 to 1837.

Illustrated by Lee Siwon

William Henry Harrison
(1773. 2. 9 ~ 1841. 4. 4)

William Henry Harrison was the 9th president of the U.S. He was born on Feburary 9th, 1773. He fought with many Indians for America. He was the first president to die during his presidency.

Also, he was the 3rd president that was a soldier. Before he became a president, he was the ambassador of the Colombia for 1year. Then, he was the president of America for one month.

Illustrated by Lee Siwo

Zachary Taylor
(1784. 11. 24 ~ 1850. 7. 9)

Zachary Taylor was the 12th president of the U.S.
He was born on November 24th, 1784. He led the U.S. to victory
in the Mexican War.

He was the 2nd president to die during his presidency. Also,
he was the 4th president who was a former soldier. He was the
general of the Mexican War from 1846 to 1849. Then, he was
the president of America from 1849 to 1850.

Illustrated by Lee Siwon

Ulysses Simpson Grant
(1822. 4. 27 ~ 1885. 7. 23)

Ulysses Simpson Grant was the 28th president of the U.S. He was born on April 27th, 1822. He led the North to victory in the Civil War. He was the 5th president who was a former soldier. Before he became a president, he was the commander of the Civil War from 1864 to 1869. Then, he was the president of America from 1869 to 1877.

Illustrated by Lee Siwon

Dwight David Eisenhower
(1890. 10. 14 ~ 1969. 3. 28)

Dwight David Eisenhower was the 35th president of the U.S. He was born on October 14th, 1890.

He led the U.S. to victory in World War II. Also, he ended the Korean War with UN. Before he became a presient, he was the captain general of World War II from 1949 to 1952. He was the 6th president who was a former soldier. Then, he was the president of America from 1953 to 1961.

To conclude, these are the six American leaders who were former soldiers. Among these six soldiers, I like George Washington the most. The reason is because he helped establish America as a country.

Part III.

Four American Presidents

Who were Assassinated

There were four American presidents who were assassinated. They are Abraham Lincoln, James Abram Garfield, William Mckinley Jr, and John Fitzgerald Kennedy.

Illustrated by Lee Siwon

Abraham Lincoln
(1809. 2. 12 ~ 1865. 4. 15)

Abraham Lincoln was the 16th president of the U.S.
He was born on February 12th, 1809. He led the north to victory during the Civil War. He was America's first Republican president.

Also, he was the first presiedent who was assassinated. He was shot by John Wilkes Booth. Before he became a president, he was a congressman of America from 1847 to 1849. Then, he was the president from 1861 to 1865.

Illustrated by Lee Siwon

James Abram Garfield
(1831. 11. 19 ~ 1881. 9. 19)

James Abram Garfield was the 20th president of the U.S. He was born on November 19, 1831. He was the second president to be assassinated. He was shot twice by Charles Julius Guiteau.

Before he became a president, he was a congressman from 1863 to 1881. Then, he ran for president for only five months.

42

William Mckinley Jr.
(1843. 1. 29 ~ 1901. 9. 14)

William Mckinley Jr. was the 25th president of the U.S. He was born on January 29th, 1843. He was the third president to be assassinated. He was shot twice by Leon Frank Czologsz. He led the U.S. to victory in the Spain War. For this reason, the United States took possession of the Philippines, Guam and Puerto Rico.

Before he became a president, he was the governor of Ohio State from 1892 to 1896. Then, he was the president from 1897 to 1901.

Illustrated by Lee Siwon

John Fitzgerald Kennedy
(1917. 5. 29 ~ 1963. 11. 22)

John Fitzgerald Kennedy was the 35th president of the U.S.
He was born on May 29th, 1917. He was 4th president to be assassinated and he was shot three times by three different assassinators. He won the nuclear war against the Soviet Union. Before he became a president, he was a senator of America from 1953 to 1960. Then, he was a president of America from 1961 to 1963.

To conclude, these four presidents made America proud. Among these four presidents, I like Abraham Lincoln the most, because he led the North to victory in the Civil War.

Thanks to
Mom, Dad, Jinny, Macy & Mrs. Park.
Written & Illustrated by Lee Siwon.

Written by Lee Siwon

Published by Chungchun Media

Designed by macygraph

Registration : July 24th 2014 (2014-02ho)

Address : Dream Venture Tower 6th 1101, Digital-ro 31gil 41, Kuro-gu, Seoul, Korea

Telephone : +82-2-801-8890

Fax : +82-2-801-8891

E-mail : stevenjangs@gmail.com

ISBN 979-11-87654-91-9